Jackie ROBINSON

Jackie ROBINSON

BY
KENNETH RUDEEN

ILLUSTRATIONS BY
MICHAEL HAYS

HarperTrophy®
A Division of HarperCollinsPublishers

Jackie ROBINSON

Chapter 1

harles Lindbergh was the first man to fly alone across the Atlantic Ocean. Neil Armstrong was the first man to step on the moon. Everyone knows about these men because they were the first to do what they did. One of the best ways to become famous is to do something no one has ever done before.

Jackie Robinson is such a hero. In

1947 he became the first black man to play major-league baseball. When Jackie stepped up to the plate to bat for the Brooklyn Dodgers, he opened baseball's doors to all black men. He played baseball in the major leagues for ten years.

At the end of his playing career any man could play baseball in the major leagues—if he was good enough. Many of the best players were black. Jackie Robinson was voted by newspaper sports writers into the Hall of Fame, the greatest honor in baseball.

But it was not easy for him to achieve these things.

Chapter 2

Jack Roosevelt Robinson was born on January 31, 1919, in a cabin that stood on the red clay fields of Georgia. He was the youngest of five children. His father was a share-cropper—a farmer who was given a share of the crops he raised for other farmers. Soon after Jackie was born, his father left home one day to look for a better job. He never came back.

Jackie's mother, Mallie, was left to take care of her family all by herself. When Jackie was still a baby, only thirteen months old, his mother called her family together.

"We are going to pack," she said. "We will pack up our clothes and some food, and take a long trip on the train."

"Where?" the children cried in excitement.

"To California," Mallie Robinson said. "Your uncle Burton lives there, and he likes it. He says we can live in his house."

The family moved to Pasadena, California, where Uncle Burton lived. Jackie's mother went to work to support her family. Jackie had always been hungry in Georgia, for there was never

quite enough food for the family. Although there was more food now, he was still hungry all the time as he grew up. Part of the reason for his big appetite was all the exercise he got. He was good at games, and he played long and hard, in school and after school.

One of Jackie's older brothers, Mack, was a fast runner. He could run faster than Jackie, and he always beat him. He beat everyone else, too. In 1936, when Jackie was in high school, Mack was chosen to run for the United States in the Olympic Games. He won a silver medal for finishing second, and Jackie was very proud of him.

Think of it, he said to himself, Mack is famous.

But not all of the neighbors were

proud of Mack. Some of the neighbors were black, and some were white, and some of the white people called Mack and Jackie names. Jackie did not understand this.

"Why don't they like me?" he asked his mother.

She could not explain it very well. Jackie also asked why the town swimming pool was only open to black people one day a week. She could not really explain that, either. But she told him that in Georgia their people had even bigger problems.

"You are lucky we live in California," she said.

Jackie was not sure. He felt angry. One day he joined a gang of boys who called themselves the Pepper Street

Gang. He liked the gang because it was made up of all kinds of kids—black, white, Mexican, Japanese.

But after a while Jackie grew tired of the gang. The boys got into trouble sometimes. They stole golf balls, or fruit from outdoor stands, and sometimes they threw dirt at passing cars. Doing these things did not make Jackie feel any happier. He decided he would go his own way. He wanted to be a good athlete like his brother Mack.

Chapter 3

Jackie's chance came at Muir Technical High School in Pasadena. By the time he was graduated, in 1937, he had played baseball, football, and basketball for his school and had run on the track team. He won a school letter, given to members of the teams, in each sport. Now Mack was proud of *him*.

Next Jackie went to Pasadena Junior

College. He worked at odd jobs to raise the small amount of money he needed for expenses. Again he played in all four sports. He became a star in all of them.

One day the track team had a meet in Pomona and the baseball team had a game in Glendale, two towns in California that are forty miles apart.

"You'll have to choose one or the other," the track coach said to Jackie. "You can't be in two places at the same time."

But Jackie wanted to go to both places.

First he went to the track meet in Pomona and broad jumped 25 feet, 6⅓ inches, to set a new junior-college record. As the crowd was clapping for him, he dashed to a friend's car. His friend tore over the roads to the baseball game in Glendale. The game was in the fourth inning, and the players were delighted to see Jackie. When he came to bat, he made two hits and helped the team win the game.

"Well, I guess you *can* be in two places at the same time," his coach said.

Coaches at bigger colleges became very interested in Jackie. One of the largest schools, the University of California at Los Angeles (called UCLA), offered him an athletic scholarship. That meant the school would pay the cost of his books and some of his meals for the privilege of having him on its sports teams. But black students were not allowed to live on the campus in those days, and so he lived at home.

At UCLA many boys compete for positions on the teams in every sport. Usually an athlete picks one sport he is good in, and sticks to that. But as the people of Pasadena knew, Jackie was special.

First he played halfback on the football team. He was quick and able to fool the other team. He carried the ball for long gains, zigzagging down the field with so many surprising changes of direction that tacklers could not put a hand on him.

"Yea, Robinson!" the UCLA crowds cheered.

UCLA's other halfback was a black athlete named Kenny Washington. He was big and strong, and good at smashing into the other team. With Jackie zigzagging and Kenny smashing, UCLA had an undefeated season for the first time ever. The fans were wildly happy.

The hardest game was with Stanford University. Jackie's team was behind

by a score of 7 to 14 when he inter-
cepted a pass thrown by the Stanford
quarterback. Before the Stanford team
could stop him, Jackie ran nearly all the
way to the end zone. His own team
promptly scored a touchdown. Now the
score was 13 to 14, and UCLA needed

one point to tie. Jackie was chosen to kick the ball to try for the extra point. He made it. He kicked the ball right between the goalposts, and the final score was 14 to 14.

Chapter 4

When the football season was over, Jackie wanted to play basketball. The basketball season had already begun, but the coach was happy to make a place for Jackie.

"His timing is perfect," the coach said as he watched Jackie.

On the basketball court Jackie was a natural. He bounced the ball smoothly up and down the polished floor. He charged in to make baskets. He danced back to defend his own goal, caught rebounds, and gracefully took the ball down the court again. People loved to see him play. He seemed to be having great fun.

Part of the reason Jackie could play both football and basketball so well was his excellent condition. Coaches told players to follow Jackie's example, for Jackie never smoked or drank. Now that he got plenty to eat at the training tables, his body was strong and fit. He wanted to keep it that way.

In the spring he played baseball, but this was not his favorite sport at UCLA. He did not do as well at baseball as he did in track. In the broad jump he won a coast championship and then the national college championship. At the end of the year honors for sports were awarded. Jackie was the first student at UCLA to win a letter in all four sports—football, basketball, baseball, and track.

However, Jackie was not content. He liked the honors. He liked the fun of being well known as a big star. But when he went home, he saw his mother still working very hard. She ironed clothes for other people and scrubbed their houses, and Jackie wished she could rest.

Also, he met a girl named Rachel Isum whom he liked very much. He wanted to be with Rae, as he called her, and have fun, but he could not afford

to take her many places because he had very little money.

"Maybe I should not go back to school," Jackie said to his mother. But she wanted him to return for his senior year.

In his second football season at UCLA Jackie was a great star. Time and again he ran down the field for touchdowns. But the rest of the UCLA team could not keep up with him. UCLA won only one game. Jackie was glad when basketball time came.

In basketball he was even better than before. For the second year he scored more baskets than any other player in UCLA's conference of big schools on the West Coast.

Just before the baseball season opened in the spring, Jackie made a decision.

"I am going to leave school and go to work," he said to his mother. "It's time I did something for you."

Chapter 5

To make money to help his mother, Jackie worked at a camp for young people, played professional football, and went to Hawaii to take a job helping to put up buildings. The place where he worked in Hawaii was near the U.S. Navy base at Pearl Harbor. He often saw the big warships and the sailors who manned them. When Jackie's job was finished, he got on a boat to go home across the Pacific Ocean to Pasadena.

"Did you hear the news?" a shipmate called to him on Sunday morning, December 7, 1941. "The Japanese have attacked Pearl Harbor! They have bombed our ships!"

Jackie thought of the naval base and the sailors, and he was very sorry. The Japanese had attacked Pearl Harbor without warning. The United States declared war on Japan. It was the start of World War II for America.

Jackie was inducted into the army. He decided to try to become an officer and he was sent to officers' training school at Fort Riley, Kansas. In time he was made a lieutenant. He was put in

charge of a group of men and tanks at
Fort Hood, Texas.

One day in Texas Jackie was riding
to Fort Riley on a bus, returning from a
trip. The driver pointed to him and said,
"You. Move to the back of the bus."

"Why?" Jackie said.

"I told you to move to the back of the bus," the driver said. "If you don't, you'll get into trouble."

Jackie refused to move to the back of the bus.

In those days in the South, black people were forced to ride at the rear of buses, while white people rode at the front. Even though Jackie was an officer in the army, the bus driver was stubborn. He reported Jackie to higher officers and got him into trouble.

It looked for a while as if Jackie might be punished. But stories were written about him in newspapers. These stories made many Americans angry. They thought it was wrong for any American to have to ride in the back of a bus, especially a man who was ready to fight for the United States. Although Jackie was court-martialed, which means he was put on trial by the army, he was found not guilty.

When Jackie got out of the army, he wondered what to do. He had heard

about the Negro league—professional black baseball teams. They played before crowds, for money. I can play baseball, he thought. I'll try it.

Jackie offered to play for a Kansas City team called the Monarchs, and he was hired. Soon, he hoped, he would be

able to earn enough money to marry Rae. She was studying to become a nurse in San Francisco and was waiting for him. But Jackie's life with the team was hard. The Monarchs played many games and traveled constantly. There was not enough time to eat proper meals or get much rest. Jackie hated the shabby hotels and the bad meals the players had to put up with.

While he played through the season, he did not dream that a man he had never met held the key to his future.

Chapter 6

Brooklyn, New York, was at that time the home of the Dodgers baseball team. The Dodgers' boss was a white man named Branch Rickey. Branch was a big man, with bushy eyebrows, and he had an honest way of talking that made people respect him. He was not afraid to be different. He was not afraid to try new ways of building a better Brooklyn

Dodgers baseball team.

At that time there were eight National League and eight American League teams. They all had only white players. Black players belonged to special black teams like the Kansas City Monarchs, but never to teams in the major leagues.

Branch did not think this was right. He wanted major-league baseball to be open to black players. He was willing to lead the way.

"Find me a great black baseball player," Branch ordered the scouts who went to games all around the country to look for fresh young players for Brooklyn. He admitted to himself that he must have more than a great athlete. He must find a man who would be brave enough to stand up to the people who liked the major leagues to be all white.

The scouts came back and told Branch that Jackie Robinson was the best black player in the United States.

"Good," Branch said. "Ask him if he will come and talk with me."

When Jackie went to the Dodgers' offices, he thought Branch wanted to put him into a new Negro league. That was what the scouts had hinted. The two men shook hands and sat down. Branch asked if Jackie was married.

"No," Jackie said.

"Do you have a girlfriend?"

Jackie told him about Rae.

"I would marry her right away, if I were you," Branch said. "You shouldn't let a fine girl like that get away."

Jackie was pleased that Branch seemed interested in his life, not just in talking about baseball.

"Jackie, I'll tell you the truth," Branch said. "There is no new Negro league. I want you to play in the major leagues. I want you to play for the Dodgers."

Jackie was very surprised.

Branch drew close to him and looked him in the eye. He knew Jackie had the talent to play major-league baseball. But he was worried. Would Jackie have enough courage in the first hard years? Like the first man on the moon, he would have to be very cautious. He would have to take one small step at a time.

Branch told Jackie about some of

the painful things that might happen. He warned Jackie that he could never fight back, no matter what names he was called or what abuse he was given.

"Mr. Rickey," Jackie said, "are you looking for a black player who is afraid to fight back?"

"I'm looking for a ballplayer, Jackie, with guts enough *not* to fight back," Branch said.

Then he told Jackie what might happen. He acted out the parts of ballplayers, umpires, and fans.

"Suppose you're at shortstop," Branch said. "I'm on the other team. I come down from first base, stealing, flying in with my spikes high, and I cut you in the leg. As the blood runs down your skin, I laugh in your face and say,

'How do you like that, boy?' What's your move?"

Jackie did not like the scenes Branch described. But he said he would try to hold his temper, try to bite his tongue, and do nothing back.

Branch was pleased. He started Jackie at a salary of $600 a month and gave him a bonus of $3,000. For Jackie that was a lot of money—the most he had ever made.

Chapter 7

That winter Jackie married his college sweetheart, Rae. In the spring he went up to Canada to play ball with a team the Dodgers owned in Montreal called the Royals. The Royals were a "farm" team, one of the many teams in baseball in which young players get experience before moving up to the major leagues. No black man had ever made it even as far as a farm team. People wondered what would happen. When Jackie got to Montreal, everybody was talking about him. Some thought there would be riots on the field. Others thought a lot of the white fans might stay away from the games the Royals played.

The manager of the Montreal team was worried. He came from the South, from one of the states where black people always rode in the back of the bus. He did not know what to think of Jackie.

Branch told him to forget Jackie's color and work for a winning season with the Royals.

What a season it was! There were no riots. Thousands of fans in all the cities where the team went came to see

Jackie play. In Montreal the fans showed Jackie warmth and affection. He got many hits—more than any other player on his team or any of the other teams in the International League. He won the league batting title. When he fielded, he made great catches. When he ran the bases, he was very fast.

At the end of the season the manager went to Branch again.

"Jackie's the greatest competitor I ever saw, and what's more, he's a gentleman," he said.

Branch liked that. But now came the biggest step of all. Jackie was going to play for the Dodgers team itself.

Suddenly life became very hard for Jackie. He and Rae had a baby and named him Jack junior, but along with

being proud to have a son, they were frightened. Some people wrote letters saying they would hurt the baby if Jackie played for the Dodgers. But Jackie had made up his mind. The first day of the season came, and he did not back down. He played ball.

Chapter 8

In the beginning many bad things happened. One of the teams the Dodgers played was the Philadelphia Phillies. The manager of the Phillies let his players call Jackie ugly names. In the heat of a game it is easy to get mad at your opponent and call him names. With their manager encouraging them, the Phillies called Jackie every name they could think of.

Another team the Dodgers played was the St. Louis Cardinals. Some players on this team said they would not play if Jackie came to town with the Dodgers. Jackie did come to town, and it was the Cardinals who backed down.

They played, and they behaved themselves fairly well.

But in many games, just as Branch
had said, players used the spikes on
their baseball shoes to cut Jackie's legs.
When he came to the plate to bat, some

pitchers threw the ball straight at his head.

Jackie was prepared for these hardships. He wished he could fight back, but, as one black man in a game controlled by white men, he knew he wouldn't have a chance. Not until he proved he belonged.

The important thing was to win. He tried as hard as he could to ignore everything else. He helped the Dodgers beat every other team in the National League. They won the pennant, the reward for being the best in the league, and went into the World Series to play against the best American League team. It was the first time in six years that the Dodgers had played in the World Series.

The next year the Dodgers signed

three more black players: catcher Roy Campanella and pitchers Don New-combe and Roy Partlow. Black men were beginning to be accepted in base-ball. That year, Jackie did not play alone.

The next year—1949—marked a turning point for Jackie. He and Branch decided that the time had come for Jackie to act like himself. If he felt like talking back, they agreed, he should do it. Jackie was glad that he could be hon-est at last. He began to talk back when he was called names by other players or by fans.

If he thought an umpire was being unfair to him, he argued with him just as any player would. If newspapermen asked him how it felt to play baseball, he

told them the truth. It was great to play the game, but from now on he was going to stand up for his rights. Jackie felt a lot better.

Chapter 9

For ten years Jackie played for the Dodgers. Mostly he played at second base, but sometimes at first base or third base or in the outfield. His fielding was excellent. His batting was excellent. He was the sort of player who could make the whole team get excited and want to play its very best.

In six of Jackie's ten years with the

Dodgers his team won the pennant and went into the World Series. People listened on the radio to the crack of Jackie's bat hitting the ball as the Dodgers fought to win. Once they did, and were world champions.

Rae and Jackie had two more children, Sharon and David. They needed more room, so they bought a house in the town of Stamford, Connecticut.

When Jackie retired from baseball in 1957, his fight was won. Black men

could play on any team in the major leagues. And in 1962, Jackie became the first black player to be elected to baseball's Hall of Fame.

After his baseball days, Jackie went into business. He became an executive in a company with a chain of coffee shops. He helped start a bank for black patrons. He advised the governor of New York on civil rights. He also traveled back and forth across the United States speaking for black people everywhere.

By 1972, Jackie was very sick. But he didn't let that stop him. He attended the World Series and threw out the first ball in the second game. It was twenty-five years after he had broken the color barrier in major-league

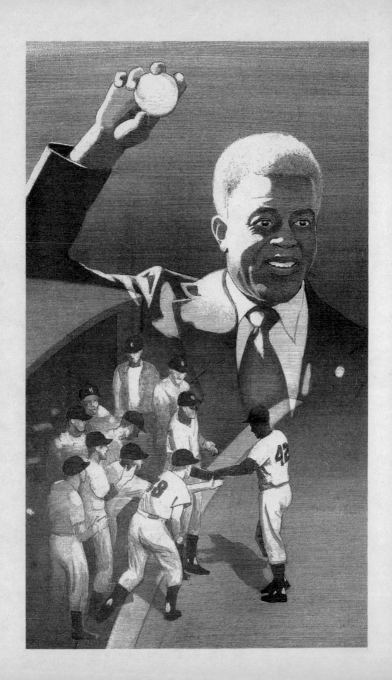

baseball. Nine days later, on October 24, 1972, Jackie Robinson died.

"We must struggle for complete equality for everyone," he always said.

Jackie Robinson lived by these words and won a great battle in the war for black freedom.

Don't miss:

Roberto
CLEMENTE

by Kenneth Rudeen
illustrated by Robert Brown

When Roberto Clemente began playing baseball in Puerto Rico, he was a thin little boy who couldn't hit very hard or throw very fast. But he practiced all the time. And in 1954, at the age of nineteen, Roberto Clemente left Puerto Rico to play in the major leagues.

His new life was hard. He was far from home, in a league where black men weren't always treated fairly. But he played on. And before long, Roberto Clemente led the Pittsburgh Pirates to victory after victory—and became one of the best-loved ballplayers of his time.

A Trophy Chapter Book

Published by Harper Trophy Paperbacks